FEEDING THE WORLD

Brenda Walpole

FRANKLIN WATTS
A Division of Grolier Publishing
NEW YORK • LONDON • HONG KONG • SYDNEY
DANBURY, CONNECTICUT

Picture Credits:
Oxford Scientific Films: cover main photo (Ronald Toms) and pages 11 top (Paul McCullagh), 12-13 (Raymond Blythe), 29 top (Raj Sing). **Bruce Coleman Ltd.:** cover small photo (Jens Rydell). **Ecoscene:** pages 1 & 24 (Sally Morgan), 5 top (Mike Maidment), 8 left (Tim Page), 15 bottom right (Ken Ayres). **Panos Pictures:** pages 8-9 (Neil Cooper), 14 (Allison Wright), 27 bottom (Betty Press). **Environmental Images:** pages 7 bottom (Venessa Miles), 21 bottom left (Chris Martin). **Science Photo Library, London:** pages 12 (Debra Ferguson), 17 bottom left (Peter Menzel), 18 (Tomasso Guiccicardini), 19 top (Cape Grim BAPS/Simon Fraser), 19 bottom (NASA), 22 and 23 (Ed Young/Agstock). **Tony Stone Images:** pages 6 and 16 (Andy Sacks), 21 top right (James Strachan), 25 top (Vito Palmisano), 25 bottom (Chuck Keeler). **Corbis Images:** pages 4 (Philip Gould), 17 top right (Hans Georg Roth), 26 (Gary Braasch), 28 (George Lepp). **Still Pictures:** pages 5 bottom (Carlos Guarita), 7 top and 13 (Jorgen Schytte), 11 bottom and 27 top (Mark Edwards), 15 top left (Peter Frischmuth). **Cafédirect:** page 29 bottom.
Artwork: Raymond Turvey.

EARTH WATCH: FEEDING THE WORLD was produced for Franklin
       Watts by Bender Richardson White.
Project Editor: Lionel Bender
Text Editor: Clare Oliver
Designer: Ben White
Picture Researchers: Cathy Stastny and Daniela Marceddu
Media Conversion and Make-up: Mike Weintroub,
       MW Graphics, and Clare Oliver
Cover Make-up: Mike Pilley, Pelican Graphics
Production: Kim Richardson

For Franklin Watts:
Series Editor: Sarah Snashall
Art Director: Jonathan Hair
Cover Design: Jason Anscomb

First published in 2000 by Franklin Watts

First American edition 2000 by Franklin Watts
A Division of Grolier Publishing
90 Sherman Turnpike
Danbury, CT 06816

Visit Franklin Watts on the Internet at
http//publishing.grolier.com

Library of Congress Cataloging-in-Publication Data
Walpole, Brenda
   Feeding the World/Brenda Walpole
          p. cm --(Earthwatch)
   Includes index.
   Summary: Looks at farming around the world and
at the global problem of providing food for all of the
people without destroying the planet.
   ISBN 0-531-14558-1
   1. Agriculture--Juvenile literature. 2. Food supply--
Juvenile literature [1. Endangered species.
2. Wildlife convervation.] I. Title. II Series.

QL83.M665 2000
333.95'42--dc21   99-056064

CONTENTS

FEEDING THE WORLD

The number of people on Earth has doubled in the last 50 years, and food production has had to grow at the same pace. Many countries produce more food than they need, but even so, many people in the world are starving.

More from the Land

There are more than six billion people alive today. To feed them all, we need to produce more food than ever before. One way to do this is to use more land for farms. About one-third of the world's land is used for farming already. More land is being cleared and planted, but this changes the environment and threatens or kills wildlife. Many parts of the world have land that will never be suitable for crops or animals, mainly because their climates are too cold or too dry.

Countries that produce more food than they need store the excess food in huge warehouses until it can be sold.

New technologies, such as mechanical milking machines, enable farmers to increase the amount of food they can produce.

New Technology

Improved technology and good farming methods help us get the best from the land we are able to use. These help give bigger and better harvests. New strains, or types, of wheat, fruits, and vegetables grow larger and more quickly, and some will grow with less water. New breeds of animals now give more milk and meat than in previous generations. Yields of food are going up year by year.

Food Supply

The world can produce enough food for everyone, but the food needs to be distributed to those who are hungry. Some countries have good farming land and produce more food than their populations need. These countries sell food to others. But some poorer countries cannot afford to pay, not only for the food, but also for the high cost of transporting it long distances.

Drought and war lead to food shortages. At this camp in Angola, southwest Africa, there are emergency food supplies from other countries. Such aid helps until farmers grow their own food again.

Eco Thought

It has been estimated that 240,000 babies are born every day. With improved medical care, many more children are reaching adulthood and living longer than in years gone by.

FARMING TODAY

Farms come in many different shapes and sizes. Animals are raised and crops grown on farms ranging from small market gardens to enormous commercial farms that use high-technology machinery.

Small Farms

All over the world, the smallest farms are run by single families. In some small farms, the farmer grows only enough grains, vegetables, and fruit for the family's needs and rears a few animals for meat and milk. Farms like these are called subsistence farms. But most of the world's small farms are run as businesses, and they produce enough surplus food for some to be sold.

Some small farms specialize in just a few crops such as grains, while others keep dairy animals or pigs. Farmers may choose mixed farming if they have different types of land that are suitable for crops and animals. In the developing world, they use animals to pull plows, to pump water from rivers, or to turn millstones to grind corn.

Organic farmers grow crops without adding any chemicals to the environment. Much of the work is done by hand.

On this small farm in Karnataka, southern India, cattle pull old-fashioned plows.

6

Larger Farms

On larger farms, all the crops or animals the farm produces are sold. Many large farms use the latest machines—for example, giant water sprinklers and combine harvesters—and some use chemicals, to boost their production. Growing grains, such as wheat or barley, is made easier by using huge machines that move and turn easily in large fields.

Modern machines do the job of teams of workers, which saves the farmer both time and money needed for plowing, sowing, and harvesting by hand. This type of farming is called intensive farming. An area of land that once produced food for ten people can now produce enough for one hundred.

This machine harvests the corn, separates out the grain, and loads the grain into a collecting truck.

Eco Thought

The average Canadian wheat or corn farm is 490 acres (200 hectares). In the Philippines, an average family farm is 9 acres (3.5 hectares). The world's largest farm, in Australia, covers 7½ million acres (3 million hectares).

Ranches

Ranches are the largest farms of all. These are enormous areas of open grassland where cattle are raised. Most ranches are in the Americas and Australia. The cattle are sold when they are young and are then fattened up on richer pasture or on controlled diets on intensive farms.

THE ARABLE FARM

We need a constant supply of some foods to provide our bodies with energy. These foods are known as staple foods. There are two main types: grain crops—for example, wheat, corn, and rice—and root crops, such as potatoes and sugar beets. Land on which any kinds of crops are grown is known as arable land.

Young rice plants are planted out in the muddy fields by hand.

Vital Foods

All staple crops are rich in starch, an energy-giving nutrient. Wheat, barley, rye, potatoes, and sugar beets are part of the staple diet in cooler parts of the world where rainfall is moderate. Millet, rice, corn, sorghum, and cassava are staple foods in Africa and Asia. These plants survive well in hotter, drier regions.

Many grains and root crops are ground to make flour for foods such as bread, cakes, cookies, and pasta.

Potatoes can be planted and harvested by machine. Potatoes originated in Peru but now grow all over America and Europe.

Rice as a Staple Food

Rice is eaten every day by more than half the world's population. It is cheap and easy to grow. Rice plants need warmth and water and grow best in waterlogged fields called paddies, mainly in tropical areas of Asia. To increase the amount of rice that can be grown, farmers and scientists have bred new varieties of rice plants. These new varieties can grow in well-drained soil in the United States, Europe, and Australia, too.

Eco Thought

In the United States an average person consumes around 3,500 calories each day. In Brazil and China the figure is 2,500 calories, while in Central Africa people eat only 1,700 calories. In the United States, only about 40 percent of the average diet comes from staple foods—the rest comes from meat and fish. In Central Africa, about 90 percent comes from staple foods.

Crops for Cash

Arable land in tropical regions is often used for crops such as peanuts, coffee, tea, tobacco, and cocoa. These are called cash crops because they are not used by local people. Instead, they are sold to make money. This money is used to buy staple foods, but many people think that poor countries would be better off growing their own food rather than buying it from richer countries.

Taking Part

Think about the food you eat. How many staple foods are there in your diet? Staple foods include not only grain and root crops but also beans, peas, lentils, and carrots.

Canada has 284,970 square miles (738,000 square kilometers) of farmland. Most of this is devoted to growing grains.

CARING FOR THE SOIL

A plant's roots take in nutrients and water from the soil. Fields that are used for crops year after year soon run out of nutrients. Farmers put nutrient-rich chemicals known as fertilizers on the soil to keep it healthy so their plants will grow well. In dry areas, fields must be watered, too.

Nutrient Cycles

When a plant dies, it rots and the nutrients, or goodness, it contains return to the soil. But when land is cleared for farming, this natural cycle is interrupted. At harvest time, crops are cut down and taken away so nothing is left to rot. To keep the soil healthy, the replacement nutrients must be added to the soil.

Crop Rotation or Fertilizers

One way to enrich soil is to let it rest every few years. After growing a grain, a farmer can plant clover, which adds nutrients to the soil. Or the farmer can follow grains with turnips, which are grazed by animals but not harvested. If this crop rotation is not possible, the farmer must feed the soil with fertilizers.

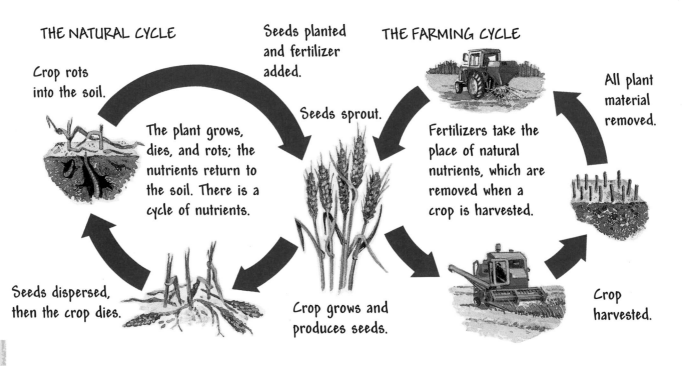

THE NATURAL CYCLE

Crop rots into the soil.

Seeds planted and fertilizer added.

Seeds sprout.

THE FARMING CYCLE

All plant material removed.

The plant grows, dies, and rots; the nutrients return to the soil. There is a cycle of nutrients.

Fertilizers take the place of natural nutrients, which are removed when a crop is harvested.

Seeds dispersed, then the crop dies.

Crop grows and produces seeds.

Crop harvested.

Feeding the Soil

Manure from animals and compost made from decaying plants are good natural fertilizers. They help keep the soil crumbly and well drained. They are used by organic farmers. Artificial fertilizers are mixtures of chemicals made in factories. They dissolve into the soil and work quickly.

Manure takes time to rot, so it is added to the soil before the crops are planted.

Watering the Land

In dry areas, farmers must water their plants. This may be done with simple water ditches dug between the rows of plants. If there is electricity, motorized pumps and sprinklers spread water over a wide area.

Soil left without water for a long time can become so dry that it blows away. Very heavy rain can be just as bad because it washes away vital nutrients or even the soil itself. Without soil, bare rock is left—and new soil takes thousands of years to form.

Soil can be ruined or trees killed by poor farming techniques such as overwatering, adding too much fertilizer, or not letting the land rest.

CONTROLLING PESTS

As much as one-fifth of all the food we grow is damaged by pests. Insects, slugs, and weeds multiply fast and can soon devastate a whole field. It is important they are killed so that crops are not wasted.

Using Pesticides

Huge fields planted with the same crop have no hedges or natural barriers to stop pests from spreading quickly across them. In the United States, the Colorado beetle is a serious pest only in large fields planted with potatoes. To keep away pests like these, many farmers spray pesticides on their crops. The chemicals they use decompose quickly after they have done their job so that none remains in our food or damages wildlife.

The best new insecticides kill only the pests and not useful, pollinating insects such as butterflies and bees. These insecticides are expensive. In many developing countries, cheaper insecticides such as DDT, which kills a wide range of insects, are still being used. They are harmful to the environment.

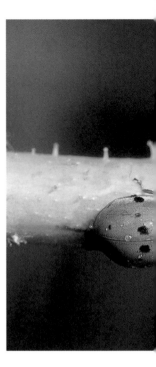

Spraying from the air ensures that the insecticide reaches all the plants evenly.

Ladybugs eat large numbers of pests in commercial greenhouses. But they are unreliable outside because they can fly away.

On the Ground

Leaf-hoppers used to be a big problem in Indonesia. The amount of pesticide needed to kill them rose every year. But when the government banned the pesticide, farmers found that natural predators took over the job of getting rid of leaf-hoppers, and their harvests increased.

Scientists in Vietnam are developing new, pest-resistant varieties of rice.

Eco Thought

There are more than a million different species of insects but only about 4,000 are harmful to crops or animals.

Natural Pest Control

Many people are unhappy with the widespread use of chemical pesticides. Cheaper, natural, and traditional pesticides are good alternatives. Some farmers plant rows of onions or marigolds between their crops because their strong smell repels pests. Natural predators, such as ladybugs, are another way of controlling some insects. Put into a greenhouse, ladybugs feed on greenfly, which are pests on tomatoes or fruit.

Outdoors, chemicals called pheromones, which are produced naturally by insects, can be a good way to lure certain insect pests away from fruit trees and into traps, or to attract insect predators. Farmers can also plant pest-resistant varieties of crops, which require no special care or treatment.

LIVESTOCK FARMING

Animals kept for their meat and milk, wool, or leather are known as livestock. Many farms specialize in rearing such livestock as cattle, pigs, sheep, or goats. Farmers choose the breed that is most suited to the land they have and the products they want.

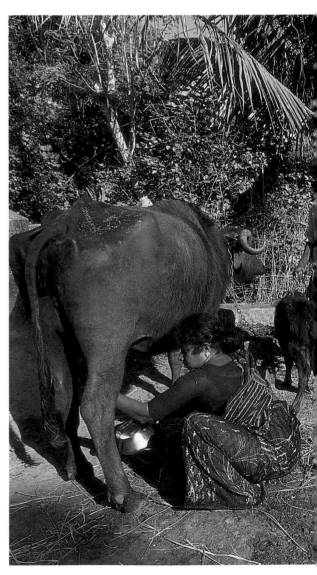

Buffalo are kept all over Asia as working animals and for their milk. Here in India, as in many parts of the world, milking is still done by hand.

Grazing Animals

Large breeds of cattle, such as Herefords, are usually kept for their beef. Smaller breeds, such as Friesians and Jerseys, are kept for milk. All breeds are kept in herds and put to graze on pastures with good, nutritious grass. In colder weather, they can be moved indoors and fed on hay or silage, which is made from cut grass, to keep up their milk production.

Sheep are hardier than cows. They can graze on poorer pasture that is too steep or dry for cattle, and no use for growing crops. Some sheep stay out on the hills all year. The largest flocks are in Australia, which has around 150 million sheep. The flocks are reared on ranches.

Eco Thought

There are more than 1,000 million cattle in the world and more than 200 different cattle breeds. In the United States, there is about one cow for every six people, while India is home to nearly 300 million animals—one for every three people.

Chickens are farmed intensively for meat. There may be 2,500 birds in each shed, where they are kept warm and fed.

Factory Farms

Large-scale, or intensive, farming of animals is often called factory farming because it gives regular supplies of eggs or meat, just like a factory. Both pigs and chickens are farmed intensively. They are kept in warm buildings and fed a controlled diet so that they grow quickly. Pigs are kept in small pens, and egg-laying chickens in single cages in huge barns where they are easy to care for.

Factory farms produce plenty of meat and eggs at a reasonable price, but many people think that keeping animals in this unnatural way is cruel. Now, some farmers rear "free-range" animals.

Taking Part

Look for free-range labels on the food in your local stores. Compare the taste of free-range and factory-farmed eggs and meat.

The Cost of Freedom

Unlike indoor chickens, free-range hens can walk outside during the daytime. They have nest boxes with perches inside and live more natural lives.

Food from free-range farms costs more because fewer animals can be kept in the same space and they cannot be fed automatically. Also, their eggs have to be collected by hand, not machines.

Free-range pigs are allowed to roam in the open and forage for their own food. They have movable shelters called arks that protect them in poor weather.

BETTER YIELDS

Humans first started to farm nearly 10,000 years ago. From wild varieties, they selected animals and plants suitable for breeding. Now, scientific breeding of plants and animals is giving better harvests and animals that grow larger and more quickly.

Better Breeds

Scientists and farmers create new types of plants and animals by growing seeds from their best plants or breeding their best animals. New generations gradually develop stronger, larger, and healthier than their parents. Today's wheat plants give three times as much grain as plants 50 years ago, and modern chickens lay more than 230 eggs each year.

These cows are about to be fertilized with semen from a carefully chosen bull. The calves will inherit characteristics of both their parents.

Not all breeding gives more food. Some plants are bred to grow where it is cold or dry, and some trees have been selected for short trunks so that it is easier to pick their fruit. As more people choose to buy lean meat, farmers are keeping animals that put on less fat.

Eco Thought

Typical modern breeds of cattle have cows that produce about 1,320 gal (5,000 l) of milk a year. However, animal breeding has produced some cows that can produce 4,226 gal (16,000 l) of milk a year.

Finding Alternatives

In Africa, local new varieties of the native grain crops millet and sorghum have been found. They grow better in the hot climate than varieties of corn, a grain crop currently grown but that comes originally from America.

Many local animals, not usually thought of as farm animals, are now being kept for profit. Crocodiles reared in Asia and Australia and ostriches in South Africa give both meat and leather. They grow quickly because they are well suited to the local weather and food.

Ostriches are now reared on farms in Africa, Europe, America, and Australia.

On the Ground

Roundup Ready corn is a genetically engineered variety that resists weedkiller. If the field is sprayed, the weeds die but the crop is undamaged. Farmers can reduce the amount of chemical they need to kill the weeds, which is better for the soil and the consumer.

Genetic Engineering

Genetic engineering is a new technique for improving plants. Genes are the tiny parts of a plant or animal that control all its features. Instead of using seeds, plants are grown in a laboratory from cells taken from a selected parent plant. Some cells are chosen to resist insect attacks; others have genes added to help them survive frost so the plants will too.

Some people are concerned that these genetically modified plants may get out of control if they are grown on farms and breed with wild plants.

Different types of corn have been genetically engineered. Scientists will test them to see which are most useful.

New Technology

Food production is a scientific business. Today's weather forecasts are more accurate than ever, and these help with long-term planning. Computers keep records and monitor production on farms and at food factories.

These scientists are monitoring a new strain of sweet sorghum. They key their findings into a portable computer.

Onscreen Farming

Computers allow farmers to plan ahead and keep records. They are used to calculate the amounts of fertilizers needed and to compare yields from one year to the next so that the farmer knows exactly where fertilizers are needed.

Using data from samples of the soil, a computer can work out which plants will thrive in which field. On large livestock farms, the animals' food rations can be formulated to give the best nutrition at the lowest price.

Weather Forecasting

Predicting the weather is essential on any farm. Today, satellites and weather stations around the world supply up-to-date, accurate forecasts. Knowing what the weather will be like in a few days' time allows farmers to plan. For example, a crop can be harvested before a stretch of rain so it is not spoiled.

On the Ground

Weather satellites are constantly feeding data to supercomputers that can do more than 2 billion calculations per second. The computers allow scientists to predict the weather weeks ahead with more than 80 percent accuracy.

This atmospheric research station provides a constant stream of vital climate statistics to weather scientists.

Using thermal imaging cameras, satellites take photographs of crops as they ripen. Here, fields of crops are grown along a riverbank. Hedges and forests appear yellow, fields of ripe crops red.

Bird's-Eye View

Satellites can take photographs of Earth from space. Onboard heat-sensing cameras scan the ground for reflected sunlight and send colored pictures to Earth. Each crop shows up as a different color, and healthy and diseased crops can be distinguished by their altered colors. The pictures help scientists assess which plants are growing well and where the soil might need more nutrients.

FARMING THE SEAS

Fishing has provided food for centuries, but modern fishing is so efficient that too many fish are caught. Unless some fish are left to breed, there will soon be none left to catch.

Fishing at Sea

Most traditional fishing takes place around the coasts, where fish come to feed. Fishing boats pull trawl nets along behind them, either close to the surface or along the bottom. They usually spend a few days at sea, then return to port to unload their catch.

Large, modern factory ships catch fish farther out to sea. They use enormous nets and haul in 100 tons of fish at a time. The fish are cleaned and quick-frozen at sea. These ships stay at sea for months, fishing night and day.

Drift and trawl nets, which can be up to 295 feet (90 meters long), are hauled behind fishing boats. They catch many fish but can also harm other creatures, such as dolphins. Purse nets are drawn up in a circle to enclose thousands of fish.

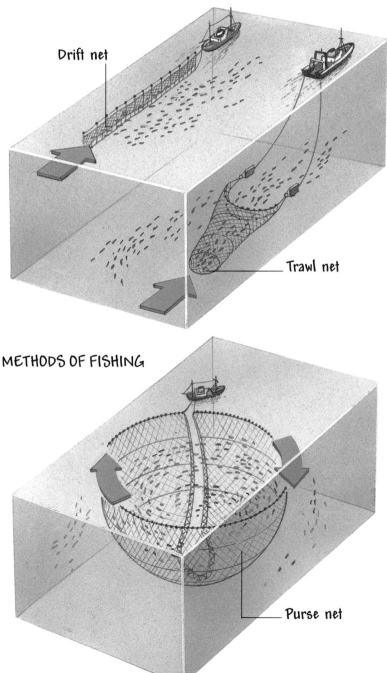

Drift net

Trawl net

METHODS OF FISHING

Purse net

Saving Fish Stocks

Factory ships catch far more than traditional fishing boats, but their fine nets trap small, immature fish. Large dragnets destroy fish-breeding grounds on the seabed. Many species are overfished and their numbers are falling. Some countries have banned factory ships from around their coasts so that the fish stocks can recover. Others have set quotas, or limits, on the number of fish that can be caught.

On a small scale, coastal fishing involves using nets that are simply held in the water. The nets trap large fish but allow small, young fish to escape.

Fish Farms

About 20 percent of the fish we eat comes from fish farms. Fish eggs are hatched and young fish transferred into enclosed, protected ponds. They are fed on a balanced diet and grow well. Salmon farming is popular in Europe, and shrimp farming is well established in Asia and South America.

Fish farms are set up near rivers or along coasts where they get a constant supply of fresh water or seawater depending on the fish or shellfish they are rearing.

Eco Thought

Records kept by the United Nations show that of 15 main fishing areas in the world, four have few fish left and nine of the rest have declining stocks. It is estimated that Japanese fishing boats catch more than 30,000 tons of fish every day.

FROM FIELD TO MARKET

Getting food from farms to stores is a big industry. Some of the work is done by hand, but most is done by machines. Using machines speeds up harvesting and preparing meat products so that food can be packed and transported as quickly as possible.

Harvesting

Most of the world's wheat is cut and threshed by combine harvesters, and now machines also harvest many other crops including tomatoes, peas, and lettuces. These machines can lift the plants, shake off the ripe fruits, and separate the leaves.

To make harvesting even easier, new varieties and strains of peas and tomatoes have been bred with fewer leaves and stems.

Journey to the Stores

Harvested fruit and vegetables are taken from fields to packing stations. Here, they are graded and packed into boxes to protect them as they travel. They may be sent to a local supermarket or taken by air to another country.

Most animals are killed close to the farm and their meat chilled before it is distributed so that it stays fresh. Many live animals are transported on long journeys to other countries by sea or road, but some people think this is stressful for the animal.

Apples from orchards are sorted and graded at this packing factory.

Crossing the World

Food may be sent from one continent to another or be carried just a short distance. Although grain and dry foods keep for a long time and can travel slowly, fresh foods need to be preserved.

To stop food from going bad, it may be chilled or frozen, but this means it must travel in refrigerated trucks or containers, which are not always available. It is expensive to ship food over thousands of miles, and many people in poor countries die every year because food they could have cannot be brought to them.

Boxes of broccoli are being loaded into a refrigerated warehouse, where they will be kept until ready for delivery to supermarkets.

Eco Thought

Harvesting an acre of rice by machine takes one person about two and a half hours. If the rice is picked by hand, 300 people would be needed to do the job in the same time.

THE FOOD INDUSTRY—many of the stages in growing and harvesting crops and getting foods to supermarkets.

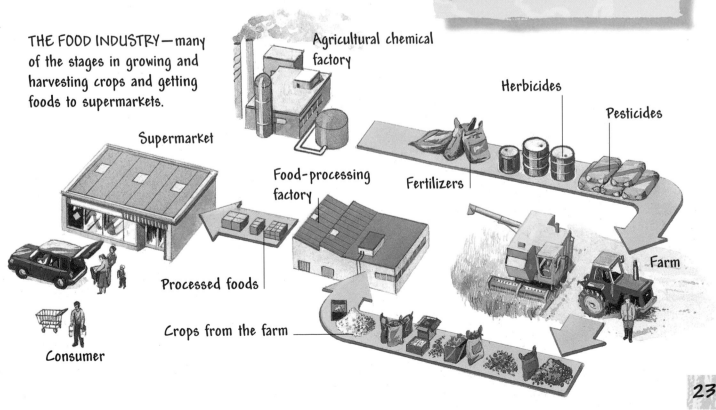

Agricultural chemical factory

Herbicides

Pesticides

Supermarket

Food-processing factory

Fertilizers

Processed foods

Farm

Consumer

Crops from the farm

QUALITY CONTROL

Everyone wants to be sure their food is safe to eat and to know how it has been processed. If food is in packages, it must be checked and labeled properly as it is produced at the factory.

On the Ground
Some fruit and vegetables are treated with chemicals so that they stay fresh longer. Always wash these foods with clean water before eating them to remove any fertilizer or preservatives.

Buying Food

In many countries, the local market is the place to buy food fresh from the farm or sea. Here, shoppers can inspect food for themselves. Food bought in stores is usually pre-packed, refrigerated, and weighed. To ensure that this food is clean, inspectors check meat, eggs, milk, fish, and vegetables at the processing factories for any possible disease or damage.

If any food producing machinery is dirty, bacteria such as salmonella can be spread and cause serious outbreaks of food poisoning. Germs can also be spread by people who handle and sell food, such as butchers and bakers, so they must wash their hands and wear overalls when they are at work.

Floating markets carry fresh food along the canals of Bangkok, Thailand, to the riverside homes of local people.

What Has Been Added?

Shoppers can check what is in their food and how fresh it is by looking at the labels. Many refrigerated foods are marked with a "Use By" date. Up to this time the food will be fresh, but after it the food may begin to decay.

The labels on processed foods must give information about the ingredients. Additives such as colorings, flavorings, and artificial sweeteners have been given internationally agreed-on code numbers so people can be sure of what is in their food. Some additives are forbidden in foods for babies and children.

Labels also show the amount of sugar, fat, vitamins, and carbohydrate foods contain. This information helps people plan their meals and avoid too much salt or fat in their diet.

An inspector checks the age of cuts of beef before they are sent to the stores.

Eco Thought

Some animal diseases, such as bovine spongiform encephalopathy (BSE), can be spread to humans. BSE may be passed in beef. As there is no cure for this disease, cows from herds where it has been found have to be killed to prevent it from being passed to people.

Check the Labels

As more people are choosing organic food, manufacturers and stores have agreed that all organic food should be clearly labeled with a special symbol. Vegetarian foods also have their own symbol, and new laws in some countries mean that any food containing genetically modified products, such as soy milk, are labeled, too.

Supermarkets regularly check that the food items they sell are properly labeled.

25

FOOD FOR ALL

Overpopulation, drought, and wars have led to food shortages in some countries. At the same time, other countries have more grain than they can use. More than enough food is produced, but much of farm produce is in the wrong place, at the wrong time.

Many tons of food, like these bananas, are thrown away each day. It cannot be kept fresh long enough to be carried to the people who desperately need it.

Food Surpluses

Governments encourage farmers to produce slightly more food than is needed so that there will be some to spare for the years when a harvest is poor. But modern farming methods mean that some countries in Europe and America produce far more than they need—every year. This food is put into stores that are already full.

Food Shortages

In some poor countries, people are starving, or suffering from malnutrition, because they do not have enough to eat. Natural disasters such as floods or drought sometimes lead to emergencies, when food has to be sent quickly from far away. Some foods, such as grain and milk powder, are easy to send, but it is difficult to send fresh foods such as vegetables and meat. These spoil on a long journey to a remote area.

It is also expensive to transport food in bulk. The cost of ships, trucks, and fuel can be too high for many countries where food is needed most.

In the highlands of western Africa, farm managers are showing local people how to build a new hedge that will help prevent soil erosion.

These refugees from the war in Rwanda, Africa, have nowhere to grow food. They have to rely on food aid to stay alive.

Solving the Problem

Food aid can help in an emergency, but a better way to help farmers in countries where food is scarce is to help them improve their land and produce more grain, meat, and milk for their communities.

Aid agencies can help with funds for digging wells and provide farm equipment and tools. They can send improved varieties of seeds that give greater yields, and they can help with irrigation to make the best use of the land. They can educate farmers to keep the soil fertile by growing crops in rotation. Using manure and compost is more sensible than relying on expensive fertilizers in many poorer countries.

Eco Thought

Hydroponics, a technique for growing crops without soil, means crops could be grown in buildings almost anywhere, even in the desert. The crops could feed people or animals.

WHAT CAN WE DO?

Everyone can do something to help people in poorer countries have a better chance to feed themselves. We can also cut down the amount of waste in our own country and do what we can to work for fair treatment of animals and the environment.

Help the Environment

We can all help the environment by buying organic products that have been produced in a natural way without chemical fertilizers or pesticides. We can also choose foods that do not have many layers of packaging. Plastic wrapping is bulky and does not break down easily when buried in landfill sites.

If you have a local farm or market, you can buy local produce and reduce the need to transport food long distances. This will cut down on the amount of vehicle exhaust gases being released into the atmosphere.

By buying free-range goods, you can ensure that many animals are reared in natural conditions.

In supermarkets, free-range and organic foods, and those without additives, are clearly labeled.

On the Ground

Some organic farmers operate local box schemes. They offer a box of local produce, at a set price, directly to the consumer when it is in season. This cuts down on packaging, transport costs, and pollution.

Fair Trade

Paying fair wages to farmers in poorer countries gives them the chance to buy better food and equipment for their farms. Many companies make sure that farmworkers who work on tea or coffee plantations are treated fairly. The companies promise to buy only from suppliers whose workers are properly paid. Look for their fair-trade products in your local stores and supermarkets.

Owners of tea plantations, such as this one in India, find that their workers are efficient only if they are properly paid.

Fair-trade goods sold in supermarkets include such products as these coffee beans and ground coffee.

Sharing and Helping

One of the most important ways we can help people in poorer countries is to share or pass on our knowledge and experience of different farming techniques, genetic engineering and food production, and hygiene. We can also help them to conserve wild varieties of animals and plants and to select breeds that can cope with or be adapted to the changes in climate that are now affecting everyone in the world.

Fact File

Working the Land

Across the world, about 45 percent of working people are employed in agriculture. In Africa, the figure is more than 60 percent, but in the United States less than 5 percent of the working population are farmers.

Specialists

Most of the money earned by countries through farming sometimes comes from just one or two crops. Denmark specializes in dairy products and Australia in wool. The United States is the leading exporter of soy beans, wheat, and corn.

Fishing Facts

The amount of fish caught at sea has increased more than four times in the last 40 years, from around 20 million tons in the 1950s to more than 80 million tons now. Such rapid growth is a threat to the remaining fish stocks.

Supertrawlers

Factory trawlers can be as long as a soccer field. The biggest trawl nets could enclose ten jumbo jets and can catch 10 tons of fish an hour.

Pig Production

In 1994, China produced 420 million pigs, about 42 percent of the world total. But the world's largest piggery is in Romania. It houses 70,000 sows.

New Crops

Several new crops have been bred in the last few years by cross-breeding. Triticale came from a cross between rye and wheat. The new variety is resistant to disease and grows well on poorer, lighter soils.

World Population

Estimates put the number of people alive on Earth today at around 6 billion compared with 1.6 billion in 1900.

Spud-U-Like

Potatoes were first taken to Europe in the 16th century and introduced into North America in the 18th century. In the 1980s 1,235,500 acres (500,000 hectares) of land in the United States were being used to grow 16 million tons of potatoes each year.

Counting Sheep

Sheep were first domesticated about 11,000 years ago. There are now more than one billion sheep in the world, kept for their meat, wool, and milk.

Watering the Desert

In the deserts of Saudi Arabia, crops are irrigated with water pumped from boreholes. These are holes that were dug down into Earth to reach oil wells. Giant rotating sprinklers are used for both watering and to apply liquid fertilizers.

GLOSSARY

Arable farm A farm that has plowed land for crops.

Calorie A unit that measures the amount of energy in food.

Cash crop Any crop that is sold for money, rather than consumed by the farmer.

Drought A long period with little or no rain.

Erosion When soil is washed away by rain or blown away by wind.

Factory farm One where animals are kept in controlled conditions to help them grow.

Fertilizers Chemicals added to the soil to help plants grow.

Free-range Describes animals that are kept outdoors and allowed to move about freely.

Genes Chemical complexes in living cells that are passed from one generation to the next and control all the processes of life.

Genetically modified Describes a plant or animal that has new genes added to give it improved characteristics.

Herbicide A pesticide that kills some or all weeds.

Insecticide A pesticide that kills some or all insects.

Intensive farm One that uses the latest machines and farming methods to get the highest possible yield.

Irrigation Watering crops.

Malnutrition When a person is weak because they do not have enough to eat or they have a poor diet over a long period.

Mixed farming When a farmer raises animals (livestock) and grows crops.

Organic farm A farm that uses only natural fertilizers and natural pest controls.

Overfishing Taking too many fish from the sea so that there are not enough left to breed and rebuild the stocks.

Paddy A waterlogged field where rice is grown.

Pasture Grassland that is used for grazing animals.

Pesticide A chemical that kills pests such as weeds or insects.

Pheromone A chemical produced by an insect that attracts similar insects for the purpose of mating.

Poultry Chickens, ducks, and turkeys kept for meat and eggs.

Quota A limit that is set on the amount of a crop to be grown or fish to be harvested.

Silage Grass that has been cut and preserved. It is used to feed animals during the winter.

Staple food A food that forms a large part of the diet of people, —for example, potatoes, rice, or wheat.

Strain A variety or type of plant—for example, of wheat.

Subsistence farm One that produces only enough food for the farmer and his or her family.

Yield How much is produced.

INDEX